Family Salt

I too have felt it behind me
as I walk: the salt of my mother!
O Let it go!

I say it again.
I want names of blooming!
Fierce! Swallowed in salt!

Family Salt

Elizabeth McKim

W

WAMPETER PRESS
GREEN HARBOR, MASSACHUSETTS

Cover photograph by Mimo Robinson.

Composition, Layout, and Design by George E. Murphy Jr.

Some of these poems have previously appeared in the following publications: *Andover Review, Black Rose, Gargoyle, Greenhouse, Grist, New Poetry 1981, The Peregrine Anthology, Ploughshares, Soundings/East, Spectrum, Thirteenth Moon,* and *The Worcester Review.*

First Edition

Inquire: Wampeter Press, Box 512, Green Harbor, MA 02041

Printed in the U.S.A.

Library of Congress Card Catalog Number: 81-51569
ISBN: 0-931694-11-6

Dedication

If you think
this love poem is for you
you are wrong
If you think
this love poem is for you
you are right
It is for all of us
who breathe into each other's life
and stand alone
See us we are the ones in the corner
See us we are the ones in the center
There someone is laughing
There someone is crying
What difference does it make
It is for me it is for you
if you think this love poem is for you

TABLE OF CONTENTS

PART I

Family 11
Baby Sister 12
Sister 13
On Seeing The Photograph Of My Father 15
I am the scar you never entered 17
I have always been 18
The Long Repetitions 19
Ma's Song 20
Aunt Bessie 21
Old Woman's Song 22
The Summer Grows Deeper 23
Witness 24
Charged 25
A Poem Of Migration 26

PART II

We Make The Love We Ride The Bus 29
To Stay Alive 33
I want 34
Creaming 35
Betty Gordon's Broad Song 36
Our Kettle Of Fish 37
I decide to go and buy a hat 38
Ore 39
Maine Migrations 40
Do you like it now 41

PART III

Our Bus Is Waiting 45
Wings 46
Movement Class At The School For The Blind 47
Archie Does The Dance 48
Poetry Class 50
About Dreaming: *Note to my students* 51
My Daughter Approaches Adolescence 52
With Jenny In Paris 53
With Jenny In St. Denis 54
With Jenny In The Valley Of The Caves 55
With Jenny In Catalan Country 56

PART IV

This Gift 59
Letter Home 60
Bro 63
Middle Age 64
Thanksgiving 65
It's Hard To Remember My Own Cracking 66
The Wonder Of It 67
Moving Into April 68
The Messages Come 70
Family Salt Raga 72

FAMILY SALT is my document of journeys, migrations, birthings, backtrackings, beginnings, soundings, ordinary emotions and motions, dances. The poems open and close with themes of family and connection: my own personal family, the family of lovers and beloveds, the family of children shaking me into the future, ready or not, the family of brothers and sisters, co-travellers in this uncertain land. The poems are informed by rhythm and pulse, breath and heartbeat, sound and silence leading me into the Common Poem which belongs to us all. This is the turf on which *Family Salt* is spilled and gathered, spilled and gathered again.

Elizabeth McKim
May 1, 1981

Part I

Family

you are
who
I am
these traces
that snowy
owl
this bud
that bed
this soft
flannel
that rough
wool
this huge
rock
that yellow
school
bus
this heart
those goloshes
that doorway
this wisteria
those bulbs
that cough
at night
that queer
lullaby

Baby Sister

You were
the last
extravagence
of the old man's
seed
You were too blonde
for me
and I was dark
and deeply rest-
less
I wanted you
to stop
and when you didn't
I held the rage
between my scabby knees
for years
Still
I wanted to hold you
Ma said
when you were born
I'd let you drop
I went away
When I came home
I couldn't hold
on anything
numbers
or colors
or even
cutting paper
I learned
to stutter
What did you expect?
A song?
Forget it
I am almost forty
I want to hold you

Sister

Your suitors
appeared at the cupboard
to taste you to show you
their mothers

My sister
you fostered the father
who loomed at the window
and waited

for lovers
to take you
his lily his valley
his daughter

My sister
you married the man
of your father's
fond dreaming

You lay in the bathroom
in morning each month
in cramps of the cradle
of woman in mourning

You trapped
your deep wishes
you left in a box
with a lock

under the bed
of your dreaming
Your sons came
like warriors

to claim you
carry you home

to their lovers
My sister my changeling

the changing is here
and it's breaking
the patterns of ever
The sunlight is healing

The women are weaving
and dancing   are reaching
their brothers and sisters
are joining the singing

On Seeing The Photograph Of My Father

When I reach for you
something falls away
I am not safe
At night I cry
In the picture you look so young
as if you can be touched
as if I can touch you

yes but
all this has happened
so long ago

I am safe
I am wearing glasses
You are not safe
You are wearing glasses
I am not safe
You are made of glass
Father
I never saw you cry

cry
father
cry

I am protected
I am wearing glasses
I see you differently
Inside the egg of a child
You loom so big
Birds fall from the nest and sprawl on the ground
I don't understand why the egg is not safe
You hold me   you do not touch me
You do not lean toward me
as I lean toward you

Father
I am your daughter
I've never seen you so masked
There are shadows around you
and the ground is wet with salt

cry
father
cry

You are taller than the trees
Our garden is enormous
No one can mow it down
You are taller than the trees
Your heels suck up the dirt
Your arms probe out the dark
You are bigger than the shadows
of the trees believe me
Father   they will not eat you
Yet

yes but
all this has happened
so long ago

I am the scar you never entered.
The one which crosses boundaries.
Which glows in the dark.
I am the touch you searched the world for.
The one you lost when you were four.
I am the shudder just before sleep
the one you forget by morning.

Believe me
if you saw me on the subway
you wouldn't look twice!

I have always been
a lonely woman
even in the beginning
not understanding the language
of men
always wanting them to see me

always hiding from them
hoping they will not crush me with their anger
trying to make them smile
with my masks
and my veils
my dancing costumes
my magic and my bells
so they would stop scaring me
so they would fall asleep
so I could take their power

The Long Repetitions

Trains in the night. In the morning waves reach
beyond water. Animal faces appear at the window
muttering cries from the pen. Fences fastened in
dirt topple over. Unafraid, the woman walks away
from the man she loves, the man who does not love
her. She is surprised at her own bravery, decides
over and over. The man cannot hear her. Preoccupied,
he repeats his own mantra which multiplies in the
lists he shreds, the prescriptions he empties. Telephone
operators listen in, unimpressed, snapping their gum
in mid-air. Below, a barrage of disco fills the street.
A step forward touches a step back. The air clears. Then
thickens. In the alley the sound of prolonged kissing. A
car honks. Its hood flies off for no apparent reason.
Shouts. A scuffle. A kick. More salt. Wounds. Nothing
is given away. Everything is shared. People complain
how the explosion continues to hurt their eyes. The long
repetitions. Trains in the night. In the morning waves
reach beyond water.

Ma's Song

All those years
Raisin the kids
Watchin em scuttle out from under
Watchin em leave
And the man stayin
Takin up more and more room
And the room growin larger for him
The room growin smaller for me
And the air blowin between us
And some days I wonder why I did all this
Why I do all this
Yet the sun comes up
The waters separate and repeat
And sometimes I know
Why I breathe
And why it has to end some day
And why

Aunt Bessie

I never knew Aunt Bessie she was a psychic medium
and she lived in San Francisco with Uncle Stewart
who wrote big books about big game hunting and
manly adventure and Aunt Bessie had séances and
made the tables rise and swell and my grandmother
when she died willed me Aunt Bessie's chinese
lacquered chest the one with swallows painted
on it and my mother told me Aunt Bessie visits
members of the family when they are hurting and you
know Aunt Bessie's in the room because you smell
overwhelming roses and there is a pressure on your
chest once when I was very sad I woke up and I felt
this huge pressure on my chest and I cried out

Aunt Bessie comes in red steam all the way from San
Francisco or further to pummel my heart out of hiding.
She gives me rooms full of roses, too many to see
or hold. The only rule: I close my eyes and smell
them through my lids. She taps on my forehead. She
unrounds my shoulders. She lets my belly go. She urges
me to fly, to touch the guardian ground and move through
any walls. I don't know her well or why she's here, but
she tames sea-lions while I sleep. She breathes on me.
She brings armsfull of loveletters from a grandfather
I never knew, a bridge builder of sorts. She talks to me
in the tongues of children. She sifts through garbage
cans and finds my mail. She combs my mother's hair because
I can't. She touches my father before he turns to dust.
She gets down on her knees to dig in his garden. She
runs over meadows to greet me. She waits for me like the best
friend I used to have. After I die, she puts me in a wheel
barrow and pushes me away. When I sleep, she puts the puzzles
back where they belong. She hums me songs. The songs
my mother knows I know.

Old Woman's Song

Saw a bee fly by my head
        it was burning
Heard my own small girl
        swallowing the sunlight
she was humming
        Lately I've been turning
to the ringing
        through the window
Today outside the springtime
        I almost tasted snow
We were frozen splinters once
        There's a bee above my head
it's calling riding
        Had a lover once
and never told my husband
        Saw his face above my bed
Heard a bell inside my head
        Lately I've been dying
for the honey in the stinging

The Summer Grows Deeper

into its circles of green
swimming in orange letting my limbs melt
Light and hot riding the waves of the season
hearing the talk of the children remembering
the girl who's my daughter a stillness
in the heart where she skips she's not here
She's visiting her husband
no i mean her father who was once my husband
it is late july hot in my place
hot in the city on the bricks
sweat-drops travelling all the way down
My body listens even the cat is gone
i wake at five want to get up leave
the apartment watch the sun
come up over the water
what a time
to be a woman
alone

Witness

The wind, a smooth unbroken rush, reaches, subsides.
The faucet in the kitchen drips apart. The cotton
curtains blow slowly in and out, filling with light.
The sound of the car motors on the street builds
and retreats, builds and repeats, echoing the sound
of the wind. Everything in my place names me. I rub
my hand against the page of the book. That too has a
texture, makes a sound. The sun moves across my
book. I see the shadow of my hand, writing. A plane
goes by. I hear the engine. I do not see it. I feel
the vibration of someone on the floor below, moving
across the floor. The wind comes up again. A small
pendant I have hung at my window taps against the
glass. I look at the notebook. My daughter has drawn
a picture for me before she went to visit her father.
I miss her sharply.

Charged

with a ragged task, I insist on going
on trips, trekking the Himalayas, past
South Station, into foreign cafeterias.
I take myself to x-rated bookstores, into
other women's bedrooms. I demand palaces
glittering with stolen jewels. I know how
to float, can breathe underwater, can re-
produce myself. My babies are endless re-
plicas. I can touch myself, know the nature
of my thirst. I have lost my baby teeth,
grin through gaps. I have a mother. She is
already orphaned. I know the shuddering of
lilacs, the closing and opening of doors, a
voice before sleep, the grief of beginning.

A Poem Of Migration

Remember I did not choose to be what I am.
Remember the deep ocean where I was born.
How I moved on the soft sands. There were
days even then I did not know who I was. I
called for my name and it did not arrive. My
body was washed with the stain of the sing-
ing. It bled in the darkness. There were birds
even then. Even in the darkness. Their sharp
songs grazed the light, asking for new surfaces,
stories of earth and air. After that we stopped
going home. We dispersed. We returned. We started
to speak, stammering at first. We became a band.
Our voices grew louder. We swarmed over beds and
shelves. We were stopped more than once. We answer-
ed no to all questions. They asked us for evidence.
We had none. Our bodies could not lie. We took
to hiding out. Some of us tried to find our former
homes, our old names. They'd been, of course, destroyed.
What can we say. The journey was long. It was painful. We
reached dry land. We were not saved. Even in the end.
Even when we arrived, our mouths
swollen, *overwhelmed* with songs.

Part II

We Make The Love We Ride The Bus

I.

we ride it
        we do not speak
we do not have to speak
        the trolley's something else
raucously cawcawing
        to paris maine to paradise
new haven what the hell
        anyway it's heaven u s a
this is the part
        where we go for broke
and I'm a working woman
        on the job by nine
when we go by foot
        the leaves squish
remember mulch
        we exist in purple
it is november
        it absorbs us
it is five o clock
        in the city
in the violet light
        we bathe quietly
slurping water over us
        out the window
someone heads across the park
        someone cloaked
I can't tell from here
        whether it's a woman
or a man
        the light pulls us
like contractions
        at the boston lying-in
there's winter ahead
        I feel it in my bones

and we haven't even
        hung up halloween
what comes comes
        I'm hoping for some warmth
short days long nights
        but we are on the freights
the landscape's speeding by
        suddenly we blank
you want to sleep
        I want to touch
animals chink-chink
        in gopher holes all night

II.

my old kindergarten teacher
        mrs. jenner squeaks by I find her
eleven o clock morning sharp
        in front of the post office on main street
she peers at me asks if I still write
        poems recalls my stutters the sandman's
assaults mrs jenner i love you
        she rubs her hands together and squints
the sun she's well past ninety nine
        and can not hear a word

III.

It's Brockton High
at lunchtime
5500 adolescents are hungry
try to find the cafeteria
all at once

hold my hand
or we'll be crushed
november leaves
grind down to nothing
in these corridors
believe me this is all Bombay

Bombay!
I can't open any wider now
Chai
The tea-man's voice assaults
the air
Chaiiiiiiiii
The scabby dog repeats

the beggars stir
kites wheel
in the beloved stink
a man chomps
off a hunk
of sugar cane
and bites down
hard
a baby flips
like a limp fish
in the heat
I smell the sun

And *you*
you're swimming in a bombay soup
of orange temple flowers
and betel juice
you disappear
in a sea of Indian faces
I catch you later this time
you're naked rubbed down with ashes

a dab of sandal wood
about the ears and you're dancing
up a *sea* of lotus leaves!

IV.

Lover
    come and touch me here
I do not blush or blur
    my legs open and grin
who knows what's going down
    or coming in

    the world speeds by
I'm eating a plum
    and you you're eating a plum
this time we're both eating the same plum
    the same plum is melting at exactly the same time!

To Stay Alive

A man and a woman
appear
each night
wearing no clothes
carrying small satchels
full of poems
outside
the wind hurts
it is january
and strong
they go to the sea
and taste salt
they go to the market
and trade the salt
for smelts
they go to the bed
and trade the fish
for love
only the most resourceful
have any chance
at all

I want:
to rub my warm soft on your face
to have you open me with yours
to flick your tongue
your deep on me, there,
I want you
to enter me behind
I want you
to put honey on me, there,
and lick it off
I want to kiss
I want to lie beside
I want to move above
I want to cup those others
in my hands
I want to for a long long time
and just before
and now at last

I want it all.

Creaming

careening
I'm roaming
over leaves and cafeterias
I'm doing a breathing boogie
through the roar of old cities
At last my friend
you see me as I am
in this half-lit room
greened and galloping

paisley skirts hiked up above my waist
sitting in this old sling-back chair
neither desperate nor dizzy
talking to you old friend
who at last will see me as I am
Don't doubt the flush of my poem
the backbone of my dreaming
This is not all puff and pulp
This is art
This is my spine
Take a look
I'm winging it now
and you can come along
Behind this mask there is none
Doors open and ache
The clam goes on strike
Morning glories give up religion
Other women join me
Turns out we are all
Revolutionary Exhibitionists!
Do you know we take baths together
slip those sponges
over all our skins
and sing for hours
It is Monday Morning
and we are not afraid!

Betty Gordon's Broad Song

I have this witch's dream
Sitting in a green garden
Our friends are sitting there
I have on a purple satin slip
I love the way it feels on my bare hot
Skin and god am I even in my inner ear
The small of my back don't tell me I can tell
Horny when I feel it and everyone is real
Laid-back I feel your fingers on my straps
I know you're going for the tits
God love em and before I can say
Mary mary quite contrary
You have released the little dahlias
I say they don't call you venus for nothin
We are all laughin includin the bobbsey twins
They're out and pink they're very unserious
You are tweakin them in front of our friends
And I am all rose and dew
My cunt's a petunia taking a bath
You know I grow crazy when you tweak the darlins
And honey I want to do the clit-dance
Rub a dub dub soaked in dew
And you are squeezin my Boo-hoo-be-doo
Pussy's croonin on key Friends are lookin
I'm tryin to be cool as if this happens every day
And I'm the pleased owner of the two titties
Of the world and no one is stranded
And I dream of lifting all seven veils
And riding you down main street
Up the great divide and me straddlin
your cock a doodle doo your thing
In me all the way back to the beginning
And a finger up the ass for luck
You singin up the moon
And me howlin down the milky way
We travel transfigured and pure
Through the throated stars till dawn

Our Kettle Of Fish

We're moving into ethers now
small places in the universe
where comets spin
and stars wink
and look at us *we're your new animals*
We roll in eel grass
We smear ourselves with seed
paint poems on our asses
We're moving in the tides now
in the world's way

on the waves's prick
on the chin of love
on top of time
spinning in the skin's sweat
we go out laughing and crying
spinning our way across a whole new life of love
an art of life
a whole work of play
a love and work
playing
a living work
loving
in the *force* of it

I decide to go and buy a hat.
I am shouting now.
I want to be loved!
You are laughing.
At a distance.
You pull something from behind
your back. It's a banner!
Mighty. Like a hat.
And then more.
Five. Fifteen. Fifty.
Fifteen thousand.
I lose count.
All around me women are smiling.
Receiving their hats.

Ore

the answer today is
there will be no answer today
even the animals won't place bets
the small caterpillar says
it may go either way

the blue heron agrees
the wind maintains
its manic dance
the trees say watch out
there is more to this
than you can know

and the rock cajoles
says don't go back
the waters are dark
the poems will drown
the child is lost
what used to be known
telephone mailbox and bush
are monsters pushing up the clay

and I don't want
my girl to know
how afraid her momma may be
or when this begins
the hard chipping at rocks
the edge we laugh on
the arduous shaping
of cloud

and the poems
how they lift me out and over
how they keep me afloat
and today I am forty
and that's not a kite or a joke
and so many texts which can't be read
where I love and let go

Maine Migrations

just that continuous push toward otherness
moving into it as into the most substantial
cloud I understand what you teach me
the simple blue of earth the eel grass
sky or its opposite and further the fish
fossil sewing its own shadows
the perfect seed asleep in silt
up to its eye the baby
dropping into the dot alone
I meet the strange beloved company
I provide myself and the fog vague
and indiscriminate touches me everywhere
All the vast moist portions of this woman's life
Not much to do in this fog but listen to it

Do you like it now
Do you
It is after all
for you
          and me
what we share
when we enter
                    from above
and below
side by side
we partake
               and penetrate
we absorb
              and are
entered
          here where
air is
      This simple
breaking of bread
                        this intimacy
                        of sky

Part III

Our Bus Is Waiting

The children are on the bus, and the bus is waiting,
and there is a garden behind the bus, and a city
surrounding the garden, and we are worried the bus
might not start, and if it doesn't start we are be-
hind schedule, and we are not sure what we will do,
or if it can be done, and how it may matter, and how
we can dare attempt it, and how we can find ways to
gain the information we need, and if there is a starting
point, and what turns along the way we have to take,
and what our mothers may say to us, and if the road goes
somewhere, and if my brother and sister are on the bus,
and if there are any maps, and if we can and our mouths
are suddenly open and no longer asking, and the children
are on the bus, and our voices are heard in the clear air,
and yes the bus is pulling out of the station the children
are on the bus they are waving the bus is moving now.

Wings

Lorenzo
Wrote a poem
About a Hitchhawk
How that bird could fly
Fly high and mean and strong
Fly like smoke
Like a terrible kite
Fly out and into light
Out doors and windows long green corridors
Basement lavatory principal's office
Nurse's room Out the center
Of the desk The bird could wing it
Teacher say This the first thing
Lorenzo here has done all year
Most likely be the last
Lorenzo smile
A high dark smile
He knew the bird could fly
He knew how wicked well
He knew how shining
Lovely was the
Flight

Movement Class At The School For The Blind

for Norma Canner

hey hello
hey hello where are you
hey hello
hey hello where are you
can you hear me
can you find me
can i touch you
will you stay
oh you have to
go now oh well
you're going
hey
you're gone
where were you
can you tell me
where are you
hey now
who are you
hey

Their eyes, rolling like agates,
their fingers pumping into palms for words,
their hands pressing the air in front of them
for possible walls, they enter, their ears
alert as listening shells, they flutter toward us
in the mute space, we have a dance, briefly;
we shuffle and slide, we touch elbows,
we caw, we flap, we wring our feet in praise;
dark fingers gather in the bell of the dance,
we laugh when they pat the hollows behind our knees
to find the beat, they reel away when the hour
is over, they leave us like a season
we can't remember how we lost.
We wonder what they know.

Archie Does The Dance

When Norma says *fist*
says *fist*, Archie doesn't want to
move, says *stop*, let's *stop*.

When Norma says *punch*, let's *punch*,
he only taps. The hot vain air
agrees it's useless. The vacuum in which
he grudgingly lumbers
says *so what*.

When Norma says *kick, let's kick,*
his feet automaticly slow down,
smother the hot red rage
into a flat
defeated
dust.

Nineteen, and black, and blind,
the institution has him marked:
retarded. Marguerite, partially blind
totally deaf, makes the sign for crazy
when he's near. When I walk beside him, he chants
behind closed doors. I hear him, his body
packed for a solitary trip.

In the dancing room the drum appears
and Archie reaches.
How do you like my odors, my odors
how do you like them he asks,
he asks, before he begins
to beat, he beats,
his mouth undoes
in a wide beatific grin
the sound of the drum takes him far
out of the class beyond the walls
into the light his packed shoulders
suddenly release his legs arch

around the drum he thrusts
his body rocks
intent and focused now
he beats the drum
his ecstatic eyes roll back
he repeats he's *getting it*
feel good he's *getting*
good it feels
getting good it feels
good
Archie's way ahead of us
it's clear
Archie's off the wall.

Poetry Class

you have to imagine
the cage you have to imagine
the room the children piling into it the fighting
you have to imagine the room and the door closing
and they coming in yelling and fighting
their high voices filling the space
and I am sitting in the middle playing a kalimba
saying *peace* and they look at me as if I speak a language
they cannot understand they converge like hungry
starlings on the colored stones I bring for them
to touch

you have to imagine
them swinging their fists
piling on top of each other you have to
imagine them crowding me and I knowing there is no more
room for them to move
and the sound of the kalimba and they say
please miss tell us how to spell
shit tell us how to spell
burn and the teacher
says *ok you guys*
if you don't want to be quiet
he is shouting now and the colored stones
are breaking I hear myself saying
don't touch the stones they'll break and a voice
from behind says *why'd you bring em*
if you don't want us to break em and one of the kids
dances over to the closet yanks out a red cloth
and a cymbal he throws his head back
he's chanting in his red cape
clanging and he's high
and sally whose brother hung himself
two weeks ago is wrapped around a poem
about a bird trying to get free
and I am sitting here
playing nothing
now

About Dreaming:
Note to my students

I too
have dreamed up a storm
toppled my father
beat someone I loved
into a bloody pulp
turned my momma into ash
changed into a one-eyed hawk
disappeared into morning
melted the mirror
I too
arrived at school without my clothes
and I have run
and remained
in the same old dirt

My Daughter Approaches Adolescence

You dance
on the dizzy edge of things
already you dream departure
as years ago
I dreamed divorce

(When I was where
you are
my momma said
go slow
she said
the water has holes in it
and the fish fall through
she said
no one should swim –
not now
with the sun on the water)

Little guest of the garden
My brown and downy mouse
I know you can swim
I remember when you came to me
from the watery place
and all I could do
was get out of your way
give you up
to the pale room
and the gloved hands

And now you will swim
Through coves and bays and open seas
You will wear water proudly
And I like a well-used anchor
will bear witness to *your* shining tides.

With Jenny In Paris

golden loaves on unknown shoulders
grandfather carp in tuileries basin
kansas couples dance with their michelins
river maid seine and up rose windows
old town sparks in morning light

child floods new as I flood older

bright red slash of woman passes
rue de seine and each day tender
crowded anemone body of roses
cherries stained with valley of tarn
camembert and gape-mouthed pigs

With Jenny In St. Denis

The print of the hand
on the face of the cave
thrown up against time
Toc! Toc!

Wild poppies
coquelicots
red and
everywhere

La gare St. Denis
Five AM
Me asleep on one bench
Jen on the other

It is cold
we dream
choco-là
café-olê

Later I scat
pre-verbal language
in front of the gare
and down dirt road

Jen asks
if cows moo
differently
in France

With Jenny In The Valley Of The Caves

and so much I feel is it the sudden welling
of time, the wound of age, the need for a companion
of touch, and my girl getting older each day, rolling
away from my care, taking her time and swiftly,
and the blinding ride between child and parent
following us, and how we will all move,
will move away again.

We visit the dark raining caves, the sweet mouths
of stone, and I who have always loved stone,
am in the magic heart of stone.

This is my journey in time. Jen asks soundlessly
how can you watch me while I grow into my new woman
while you are busy kissing? What to do, and I grow
older, grey in hair, hands disappearing into the vast
landscape which shall finally possess me, and I shall
finally let go. The swallows circle.

On the cave walls we see the bison, the caribou,
the reindeer, the elk. Once the land was tropical.
Hippopotomi grazed. I feel the first traces of people,
their scrapings, their prayers and magic, their reminders
flung up against a wall. Who will come after, who
will come? The cries of swallows. The child growing.
Night folds into day. Hot. We blossom in cave flowers,
their dark interiors, their dyes, their traces, a hand
thrown against a wall, dark dreams chanting as the magic
covers us, as we climb into the heart-stones, as we
listen for the snufflings of the beast.

With Jenny In Catalan Country

as real as cheese
as fine as wine
coup de rouge
mud in your eye
up yours
down your mother's
today's a day
like any other

The wind blows off the Pyrenees
each night we settle in
chat eau oh oh

ch ch ch urch
sh sh sh
ahtoe ahtoe
I forget what language I speak
clear green words appear
at the floor of my mouth

The wind caresses the sky
here where bare-breasted women
and children loll in the sun

catalan catalan
in the square
they dance sardanes

The kid tells me
I stagger
after a quarter liter

well so I do
So I do

Part IV

This Gift

Transforms itself into a key for you. This key
can stand on its legs, can talk with beasts.
This key knows the smell of its own body. This
key has found such friends, such beauties, this
key has tasted the tears of others like it, this
key can breathe.

This key begins to dance. This key has known
the dances of friends and praises their motion,
their salt. This key has known the beatings
of birds, the wings of friends, their beatings.
This key transforms itself into a gift for you.

I want you to know the heavy burden of this gift,
this bastard of a present, this bitch. I want
to give you this, you whom I have loved. I want
you to take it gently and blow it from you like
milkweed, like weedmilk, like mother, like magic,
like numbers, like the song of ourselves, like
our song of passage, our power,

our salt. O look! This small thing is my gift:
You whom I love so dearly:
my gift.

Letter Home

(Hello
hatchet-faced scots
castillians from st. petersberg
all you old oppressors conquistadores
slave owners capitalists effetes aesthetes
doctors psychic mediums nervous breakdowns
presidents of chemical companies up country millers
pillars of the community
ladies of breeding
etc.)
hello hello
father pushing up the loam
chopping down the brush
burying the rock
hello mother feeding catbird and evening grosbeak
hello father tending blood root and hepatica
hello mother wrapped in grey flannel
seasoning the rice with subtle herb
sipping gin in slow sighs
keeping in the gentle
keeping out the wild
just recently I dreamt I saw you Ma
dancing on the cliff
where I have done the dance
and you were laughing
It reminded me of when I was four
and you dressed up as a witch
and I was scared
I come to sit beside you
I come to tell you
Soon we will die.
That much is sure.
Fighting is everywhere. Countries are at it.
And on every street corner. And in the stairwells
of schools. And at their entrances
which are swallowed up by cop cars,

they are asking now for metal detectors.
Blood is everywhere.
Even your granddaughter is worried.
At fourteen she has just begun to bleed.
The free tampons which were bounced
on our doorstep, the ones she has used
since the bleeding began
can cause her death.

Today it is raining.
I am alone.
My child and my lover are away.
She is visiting her father in Vermont
and he has gone to see his little girl
in Pennsylvania. I am writing to let you know
I am happy
that life with this man is uncommonly good
that we share love together
Each night he holds me
and we pass messages
through our skin our mouths
and the soles of our feet
He smokes cigars and dollops his coffee with brandy
He listens to Illinois Jacquette
and Dakota Staton
He sings 'Sylvie Sylvie I'm So Hot And Dry'
He says his nose is open
and we laugh about that
now that I know it means I turn,
and turn him on.
I have visited his family.
We have shared food together.
They come from the flatlands
of Kansas and Nebraska.
They have Creole blood in them and Indian too
and African. I tell them I also come

from proud people. But how are they to know.
At night this man holds me
and enters my life.
The child the man and me
we are trying to make it work.
It is not always easy.
I write to let you know my news.
My friends are a family.
They welcome us.
I miss you.
The granite face the hack and fuck of water and rock
the call of cormorant cutting into
shoulder blade.
Lately I have opened up so much.
I have glistened and I am not afraid.
My work is moving into new levels.
How are you?
I love you as always your daughter Elizabeth

Bro

My brother
I have never seen the sun
so bare and near
just me and it
without *your* light and shade
and now I want to name it
for my own
so long
so long time comin' bro
the names roll into me
like seed like skim like salt
like skipping stones like skin
like loveliness one's own
like names
like *lisa lara dolorosa mara*
like *paolo raffael venanziano*
like *ed* and *robert*
judith
sun like stone
water like hole
the names are popping out of matrix now
beginning blossoming
we want them now
leaf on leaf in millions
brothers onto sisters named
and changing
in the open air
We want to wash ourselves in them
In sun let water lightning slide down flanks
Let roll and cry and come apart
Together fly let go
Let looser now let go
Let laughter loose let silence into air
Let be Let go

Middle Age

A shapeless wordless being
halfway out of a dream
halfway into a life
halfway in a hole
and deciding to hear to be heard
and in the middle of a great wind
in a crazy dance and the decision not yours
not mine but halfway into a restless body of water
animals coming in for a landing
and water slightly shaking holding up a mirror
and the birds coming home
red birds the color of blood and the sound
of great rivers *ganga mississippi rio grande*
pressing near the door
opening to a pulse
a heart I only half hear
and a young half-grown woman
afraid and dancing in the wind
and the press of soft skin in a circle of light
and the dawn bends and arches in a rush
new voices bringing in the day
and from far away
a shapeless wordless being
halfway out of a dream

Thanksgiving

How did I know
you were going to start out shaped
like this, pinned to the moment,
trembling like silk in the wind,
how did I know what the roar in the ear
would do to the hearing, what the lights
of the traffic would mean, how did I know
that troubled, I would sing like a stone,
that the day would fold back a million answers
into the ring, that bells would expand like the throats
of divas, that men wearing ten gallon hats would appear,
that someone would declare a holiday, that someone else
would declare an open bar, that bawdy songs
would rise up and mix with hymns of praise,
that the aunts and the uncles would do a slow polka,
that stalks of cat o'nine tails would sway, solemnly,
that my mother would begin to cry, softly at first
and then full flood, that bread would be broken
and cheese and melons would start to nod,
that wine in its vintage would acknowledge us,
that someone would sprinkle poppy seeds on all our heads,
that flags and peonies would begin to gape,
that Rector Harding from our town would arrive
without his clothes, his enormous belly a beacon
glowing, that a troupe of snowy egrets would
stick out their tongues, and that you
and I would look at each other
and begin to laugh.

It's Hard To Remember My Own Cracking

and how I asked for pictures, more pictures
and suddenly I felt appetite
and I knew I was going to travel
I was a singing creature among many
my spine was released by bells
I experienced melting and multiplying
I wondered if it was worth it
when you came I couldn't remember your name
though you had filled my dream
the windows were knocking
the doors became transparent
light poured in
the amazed fish joined and jumped
there was somebody playing the tuba
at which point the whole damn high school band joined in
a chorus of frogs offered themselves up
out of ponds, and in a place I could only know
with the soles of my feet, I up and started
to dance; and we danced down long corridors of childhood
and lost light years of easter, and all of our bodies
moved into the new season which was suddenly
ours.

The Wonder Of It

Moving out and up with no help from an alphabet.
No eyes behind our head. No seeker and no path.
A weight. A time for everything. The woman opens
to the man. The man does not stop to wonder why.
What green we can lie down in, we do. It is as
simple as that. The forest walks off the farthest
corner of the stage dragging its own tree. Somewhere
a man on a motorcycle at the edge of a highway takes
a siesta. Nothing is flattened. Not yet. There is
green enough for everyone. An arena in which we can
play and weep and be ourselves. Somewhere I see a
door. Wind both inside and out. There is love here.
Open. Timeless. Standing straight up. There is a jar
being toppled. Turned inside out. There are two paths
converging. Beyond that, the sea. The smell of the
creatures after they have moved on. The warm spot on
the picture where they lay down together and dreamt.
How they danced the sweat of their vision and then
forgot what they had seen. Somewhere someone is
touched. That is all we know.

Moving Into April

holes
in the waterbed
a wet seep
I wake up
in a swamp
of feeling

Yesterday
I bought purple tulips
wax pilgrims at my window

the buds are back
on my own tree
a faithful lover
in storms
all night tapping

I love your daring
and your daring do
sure do hope
you love
my doo dah
doo dah

manifest me
manifest me
all night long

Simple man
and simple woman
sitting in the simple sun
waiting for the simple night
when they can make
the simple fun

I keep tryin
to push through
constant

re-creation
as the time allows

I feel in the middle
between this and that
pushin through
doin the breast stroke

doo dah
and at night
I dream the Connecticut Valley
in mid-august-fire-
flies everywhere

Pack up your sorrows
in your old kit bag

What I want is some clarity
What I want is some light

When I lay down with you
I brought in
a whole pack of sorrows
and some joy
Can't say I didn't want it

and good work
to follow me
all the days

I feel your song now
singin in the empty street now
On retreat now
Sing it sweet now

Binga banga
ringa ranga
finga fanga
gotta go now
singin low now

The Messages Come

A host of black children
in Atlanta turn
and the new light fades
in the crumbling land

eight minutes
eight minutes to midnight

If you love the earth
If you want to live
If you have to love
The messages come
A call to live
If you want to love
The messages come
There is no choice
If you love the earth
The messages come
Bearing down
In the turning year
The messages come

With release
With soundings
Full with bullets
And ripped flesh

Full with muggings
And crushed spectacles
Tears mark the place
Where the messages come

Full with the buds in their breaking
Full with the swamps in April
And gossamer mornings
The messages come

Full with ladders which can deceive us
Full with half-finished work

And full with a voice which needs to sing
Full with the beckonings of babies
And full with the unanswered belly
And the flight of crows
The messages come

Full with the half-chewed morsel
And the heavy birthing crowds
And the dawn of moon and tendril
Full with the loss of you
On this day of newmowing
The messages come

Family Salt Raga

Falling at exactly the same time
the down and come-down of the same golden hoard
the red endings, skitterings into mulch,
racing toward the cold, the white takeover,
the silence of crows, days given over to heat,
the fire in front of my eyes, and behind me my mother,
and behind her, her mother and all of us moving
into the same frosted autumn air
the procession even, and a shadow
for each of us as we walk,
a shadow to make us disappear and a shadow
to make us larger than life
and the cloud moves into green
(what was given suddenly bends again
toward earth) red everywhere:
leaves, farewells, fur, hallways
and the quiet sleep all wrapped up and covered over
some say protected, touching the salt-seed,
the kernal knowledge, lost towns,
treats, windows, bakeries,
groceria, hands touching tokens,
tokens turning silver in the dusk-light,
the salt carrying us over and over
into remnants, and larger portions, now behind me
a glimpse of glass, the boss leaving home and mary,
little lamb all tumble down,
sing a song of six
particles, salt
in the wind
and ever
so shy-
ly stir
wish slip and heaven
the red place a hunch
an approach and more eating
stuffed towered over
a trampoline heaving

a fine line
fire lane
a lingering
huffing
let up, let up
we were only asking for spring
a spring sparing no one
silk whispers in all our parts,
in the blinds, behind the partitions,
windows going up, tulip-knowledge, spring-
board into green flood, narcissus,
pop of blossom, kiss in the moist suck,
eels and the watering stones,
mortuary and the dark cloths,
dirt fill hole
prayer and oh no
oh ho and yay oh
mourning and swaying
cover recover the baby
the warming of flowers
the flowing of salt unveiling of stone
the bleeding of hours, the warning of seed-law,
ritual endings return to the natural weathers
winsome and glowing handsome and feathers
heavy all day assuming and roving
dozing in sun-high
late spring of the mud day the dog day
spring into summer like velvet
like salt talk like fucking
and licking
sluicing
god mud
mud and the sweet pig
tomorrow sweet mama blazes and ointment
oaxaca the oranges market the turn in the here-spin
factory noon place dark weight the fulcrum
beginning and flying home into knowing

the fleeing and crawling and dying
the lifting and rising the raining and shining
the breathing and drying the owning
family salt unfolding the light
sifting and spreading dreaming and shifting
family salt unfolding the light
family salt unfolding the light

Elizabeth McKim, the Boston-based poet was born in rural Connecticut in 1938. She has read and performed her work widely, and has collaborated with dancers, musicians, and visual artists. Her poetry has appeared in many magazines. She is included in a Pomegranate Press chapbook of women poets entitled *New Poetry*. Her first collection of poetry *Burning Through* was published in 1978 by Wampeter Press and The HOT MAMA POETRY COLLECTIVE. She directs workshops for people of all ages involving movement, sound, and language, and is a member of the Faculty of the Arts Institute for Expressive Therapies and Integrated Arts at Lesley College in Cambridge, Mass.